3·15

W9-BOM-988

A Kid's Guide to
THE MIDDLE EAST

Understanding
TURKEY
Today

TURKEY

Alicia Klepeis

Mitchell Lane
PUBLISHERS
P.O. Box 196
Hockessin, Delaware 19707

Understanding Afghanistan Today

Understanding Iran Today

Understanding Iraq Today

Understanding Israel Today

Understanding Jordan Today

Understanding Lebanon Today

Understanding Palestine Today

Understanding Saudi Arabia Today

Understanding Syria Today

Understanding Turkey Today

Turkey

Edirne
Kirklareli
Kesan
Istanbul
Eceabat
Bandirma
Canakkale
Bursa
Bilecik
Balikesir
Kьtahya
Eskisehir
Manisa
Usak
Izmir
Aydin
Bьyьk Menderes
Denizli
Burdur
Bodrum
Mugla
Marmaris
Antalya
Karaman
Gazipasa
Silifke

Izmit
Bolu
Adapazari
Sakarya
Ankara
Kirikkale
Afyon
Isparta
Konya
Beyseh Gьlь
Tuz Gьlь
Nevsehir
Nigde
Eregli
Mersin
Tarsus
Iskenderun
Antakya

Inebolu
Sinop
Karabьk
Zonguldak
Kastamonu
Cankiri
Corum
Kizilirmak
Kirikkale
Yozgat
Kirsehir
Kizilirmak
Seyhan
Ceyhan

Samsun
Carsamba
Amasya
Yesilirmak
Tokat
Sivas
Maras
Gaziantep
Urfa

Ordu
Giresun
Trabzon
Rize
Gьmьshane
Coruh
Erzincan
Tunceli
Elazig
Malatya
Diyarbakir
Adiyaman
Tigris
Akcakale

Artvin
Kura
Kars
Aras
Karakьse
Erzurum
Bingьl
Murat
Van Gьlь
Mus
Tatvan
Bitlis
Ferry
Van
Siirt
Kurtalan
Batman
Hakkari
Mardin
Nusaybin

TURKEY

SYRIA
LEBANON—
IRAQ
PALESTINE
ISRAEL
JORDAN

AFGHANISTAN

IRAN

SAUDI
ARABIA

Mitchell Lane
PUBLISHERS

Printing   1   2   3   4   5   6   7   8   9

Library of Congress Cataloging-in-Publication Data
Klepeis, Alicia, 1971–
Understanding Turkey today / By Alicia Klepeis.
    pages cm. — (A kid's guide to the Middle East)
Includes bibliographical references and index.
ISBN 978-1-61228-649-5 (library bound)
1. Turkey—Juvenile literature. I. Title.
DR417.4.K56 2015
956.1—dc23

                                                                        2014009360

eBook ISBN: 9781612286723

PUBLISHER'S NOTE: The fictionalized narrative used in portions of this book are an aid to comprehension. This narrative is based on the author's extensive research as to what actually occurs in a child's life in Turkey. It is subject to interpretation and might not be indicative of every child's life in Turkey. It is representative of some children and is based on research the author believes to be accurate. Documentation of such research is contained on pp. 60–61.

The Internet sites referenced herein were active as of the publication date. Due to the fleeting nature of some web sites, we cannot guarantee they will all be active when you are reading this book.

To reflect current usage, we have chosen to use the secular era designations BCE ("before the common era") and CE ("of the common era") instead of the traditional designations BC ("before Christ") and AD (*anno Domini,* "in the year of the Lord").

                                                                                    PBP

CONTENTS

BOLD words in text can be found in the glossary

Introduction

Turkey is a fascinating country. Located at the intersection of Europe and Asia, Turkey has been influenced by people and ideas from both continents. Turkey's history, food, and political system all reflect this mixture of East and West. Like many countries in the Middle East, Turkish history has seen conflict over the centuries. Even today, different political groups in Turkey don't always see eye-to-eye on the country's future.

Turkey faces challenges in the twenty-first century. Sharing water with its neighbors is one issue. Dealing with earthquakes is another. Helping its Syrian neighbors who are in the middle of a civil war is also difficult. Yet the Turkish people are creative thinkers. They have used Turkey's resources to develop industries and start new businesses. Farmers here grow food that is eaten

Istanbul at Sunset

not only at home, but also by people around the globe. From preschools to universities, Turkey offers wonderful educational opportunities to its people.

Family and culture are very important to the Turkish people. Dancers, musicians, and writers create beautiful works of art. Like many Middle Eastern nations, most Turks are Muslims, or followers of Islam. This religion plays an important role in peoples' lives. Families worship, celebrate holidays, and share meals together. Kids and adults in Turkey play sports, watch movies, and enjoy games—just like you do. From the mountains to the Mediterranean Sea, Turkey is a beautiful land with much to learn about.

A typical breakfast in Turkey

CHAPTER 1
Turkey—A Day in the Life

Merhaba (MER-ha-ba)—Hello! My name is Kerem. I am twelve years old. I live with my mother, father, and little sister Kayra in Istanbul, the biggest city in Turkey. Our apartment overlooks the Bosporus Strait. That's a narrow strip of water that flows through Istanbul and separates Europe from Asia.

On a normal school day, I wake up around seven o'clock in the morning. I like to eat eggs, olives, and some bread with cheese and ham for breakfast. I always look forward to my cup of tea with breakfast. In Turkey, tea is called *çay* (pronounced "chai"). It is strong black tea. I like mine with sugar. After I eat, I put on my school uniform. Since my grandmother lives in another apartment in my building, she comes to watch Kayra while my parents get ready for work. My mother is a tour guide and my father works in one of the big hotels downtown.

Before I walk down the block to meet my friends, I make sure I have everything I need in my backpack. We always walk to school together. It only takes about ten minutes to get there. Sometimes we start talking about wrestling or movies. Then it takes a little longer.

My first class starts at nine. I study history, science, math, Turkish, and English. There are about thirty kids in my class. My cousin Talya lives in the Turkish countryside. She has over fifty kids in her class! My favorite class is phys ed. I love when we play volleyball or soccer. Sometimes during the ten-minute break between classes, I go to the cafeteria and buy a snack. I usually buy *simit*—bread rings covered in sesame seeds.[1] Yum!

I walk home for lunch halfway through the day. My grandmother makes my lunch. Some days we have cabbage leaves stuffed with rice and chopped meat. Other days we have soup with rice and meatballs. My favorite lunch is *pide* (PEE-deh). It's like a flatbread pizza with vegetables, meat, or eggs on top.

Kerem attends school in Istanbul, where many students wear uniforms. These seventh-grade students are getting ready to begin their English class.

After lunch, I walk back to school where I have classes until three o'clock. I often go to study hall after school to get my homework done. I want to do well in school now so I can get into a good high school. I really like science and I want to become a biologist. My friend Deniz loves English. He hopes to study at a university in England when he's older.

When I'm back home and my homework is done, I can have some fun. I change out of my uniform and head to the park to see my friends. Some afternoons we play soccer, dodgeball, or basketball. Other days we play marbles or tag. We often run into the girls in our class at the park. They like to play double dutch, hopscotch, or volleyball.

After my mom and dad get back from work, my grandmother heads back to her apartment. Some nights she'll come back to join us for dinner at around eight o'clock. Dinner is the biggest meal of the day. We usually have some soup or salad first, then lamb or chicken with rice and vegetables. And for dessert? Most nights we have fruit. I like pomegranates, figs, and apricots best. But my favorite dessert is *lokma*—round donuts in syrup.

When dinner is over, I watch television or play a computer game. Some nights I prefer to read a book. Lights are out in my room by ten.

IN CASE YOU WERE WONDERING

What sports do people play in Turkey?
Most **Turks** enjoy a variety of sports. The most popular sport in Turkey is definitely soccer. Basketball and wrestling are also well-liked. Have you ever heard of oil wrestling? It's a Turkish sport where the competitors cover their bodies in olive oil before they wrestle. This makes it hard for the wrestler to get a grip on his opponent. In the mountains of Turkey, people ski. People also enjoy swimming and scuba diving at Turkish beaches.

IN CASE YOU WERE WONDERING

How long do kids have to attend school in Turkey?
The Turks place a high value on education. There are five stages in Turkey's public education system: preschool, elementary school, middle school, high school, and university. Preschool classes are optional for children ages three to five. In March 2012, the Grand National Assembly (Turkey's parliament) passed an education reform bill. This bill extended the length of required education from eight years to twelve years. Kids' primary education (elementary and middle school) begins at age six and continues to age fourteen. Four years of secondary education (high school) are now required as well. Starting in middle school, students may attend general academic schools, or they can choose a technical or vocational school that specializes in fine arts, religion, science, or foreign language.

On Sundays, we usually get together with my whole family. I have lots of cousins, aunts, and uncles. My father's parents live on the other side of the Bosporus Strait, so we take a ferry to visit them on the weekends. My father's mother, whom I call *Babaanne*, always cooks up a feast. She makes the best *kabak tatlisi*, which is a sweet pumpkin dessert with walnuts. My grandfather likes to play **backgammon** or a tile game called *okey* with us. Kayra and I look forward to Sundays every week.

I hope you enjoyed reading about my life here in Turkey. *Hoşçakal* (hoash-CHA-kahl) Goodbye!

Okey

WHAT'S TO DRINK?
BEVERAGES IN TURKEY

From breakfast to bedtime, Turks have a wide variety of drink options. Juice, tea, and coffee are all popular choices. Tea, also known as çay, is appropriate any time of day. Turks brew it in a large urn called a samovar. Normally, tea is served in tulip-shaped glasses. Turks take sugar in their tea, but not milk. Stopping in to visit a friend? She'll offer you tea. Looking in the window at a shop? The owner might offer tea to a customer to get him into the shop. People in Turkey often enjoy mint, rose hip, apple, **linden**, or lime flower teas.

A samovar and tulip-shaped glasses make teatime feel special.

Turkey is also known for its coffee. Called *kahve* (kah-VEH), Turkish coffee is strong and somewhat bitter.[2] Unlike Americans, who often drink very large mugs of coffee, people in Turkey enjoy their coffee in small cups. It is typically found on the table with dessert. People often add sugar to their coffee as it's made. And the grounds at the bottom of one's cup? They get left behind.

It's interesting to note that traditionally, women have had tea and pastries at home, while men were more likely to meet up at a local coffeehouse. Most Turkish women still do not go to coffeehouses in rural areas. In cities, however, both men and women can be found at the corner coffeehouse.

Do Turks drink juice? You bet! Orange, pomegranate, cherry, and apple juices are all popular. During the winter, Turks may enjoy some traditional beverages. *Sahlep* is a hot drink made from orchid root. It's served with cinnamon. Another Turkish beverage is *boza*, which is made from fermented wheat.[3]

Istanbul is the largest city in Turkey. A global city, it is also the nation's historical, cultural, and economic center.

CHAPTER 2
City and Country Life in Turkey

Do all Turks live in the same way? Of course not. People's lifestyles vary throughout Turkey. About 72 percent of Turkey's **population** lives in cities.[1] Turkey's biggest city by far is Istanbul, with over ten million residents. Other major Turkish cities are Ankara, İzmir, Bursa, and Adana. Most Turks who live in cities have service jobs. They work in schools, offices, hospitals, restaurants, and shops. Turkish cities also have many factories. Factory workers make cars, **textiles**, metal goods, and food products. Turkish city dwellers can visit excellent museums. They have many schools and universities to choose from.

How do people in Turkey's cities get around? Some people travel in their own cars. Turks also take shared taxis called *dolmuşes.*[2] Dolmuş means "stuffed." The name is especially fitting during rush hour, when many people are dropped off and picked up.

Turkish urban areas face some challenges. One is a housing shortage. As people leave the countryside to settle in cities, there aren't enough places to live. People have created shantytowns outside the cities. The Turks call these areas *gecekondu* (GEH-jeh-KOHN-doo), meaning "built in the night." Sometimes these dwellings are connected to the main electricity supply. If so, some gecekondu residents can use appliances like televisions or refrigerators. Finding work can be another difficulty for urban Turks. New city dwellers don't always have the right skills or connections to get a job quickly.[3] Fortunately, Turkey's economy is growing.

Shantytown in Ankara, Turkey

About 28 percent of Turks live in small towns or villages. The pace of life here is usually slower than in the cities. Walking out from his stone house, a rural resident might tend to his family's sheep and olive trees. Most Turks in the countryside make a living by farming. Some grow cash crops including tea, hazelnuts, sugar beets, grain, or cotton. Farmers often raise livestock. Sheep, goats, and cattle are most common. Some rural Turks earn a living by working in mines. Coal, iron ore, and copper are a few of the natural resources that are found under Turkey's soil. Today more people in the Turkish countryside have cell phones and Internet access. This allows rural dwellers to be more connected with the rest of the country—and the world.

Family is very important to Turkish people. Family members living in Turkish cities commonly rent apartments in the same building. In the Black Sea region, Turks might live in cottages near extended family members. Other rural families have extended family living under the same roof. It's not unusual to

Coal power generator at Nallihan, Ankara, Turkey

A grandfather plays marbles with his grandsons at a park in Istanbul, Turkey.

have grandparents, adult children, and grandchildren living together. Nearly all unmarried adults live with their parents. Elderly relatives often move in with their children instead of going to a nursing home. Extended families regularly share meals. Holidays also provide opportunities for people to celebrate with one another.

IN CASE YOU WERE WONDERING

What holidays do people celebrate in Turkey?
Turks celebrate both public and religious holidays. Many of the public holidays mark the most important days in Turkey's history. The Turkish parliament, called the Grand National Assembly, was established on April 23, 1920. To honor this event, National Sovereignty and Children's Day takes place every year on April 23. How do people celebrate? They wave Turkish flags, have parades, dance, and recite poems. Children even take over the Grand National Assembly for the day.

THE SUGAR FESTIVAL,
OR ŞEKER BAYRAMI

One of Turkey's most beloved religious holidays is *Şeker Bayrami* (shay-KAIR BYE-rahm). It's also called the Sugar Festival. (Şeker means "sugar" or "candy" in Turkish.) This three-day holiday marks the end of Ramadan, a month-long period of Muslim fasting. People prepare for this festival by cleaning their homes. They shop for food, gifts, and new clothing. They also give a donation to the poor to ensure that everyone can enjoy this celebration. On the first day of Şeker Bayrami, people wake up and wash themselves, and eat breakfast. They often put on new clothes. Most Turkish men head to the **mosque** for their morning prayers. They then return home to celebrate with their families.

Şeker Bayrami is a time to visit relatives. During the Sugar Festival, people visit the oldest members of their family. Adults visit their parents and grandparents. Turks will visit the cemetery if their relatives are deceased. They spend time with both close and distant relatives. The person being visited offers his or her guests a variety of sweets and confections. Adults give both sweets and money to children.

How else do people celebrate this "sugar" holiday? Some Turks celebrate in a more traditional way. Elders might dance to music, or oiled wrestlers might have a match.

People celebrate the end of Ramadan on the Golden Horn waterfront in Istanbul, Turkey.

A crowd of Muslim men pray in the Süleymaniye (soo-ley-MAH-nee-yeh) Mosque. The largest mosque in Istanbul, it is one of the city's most spectacular landmarks, featuring beautiful stained-glass windows, enormous columns, and detailed tilework.

CHAPTER 3
The People of Turkey

Turkey is home to more than eighty million people. These people belong to different cultural and ethnic groups. Each group has its own beliefs, traditions, and customs. Still, Turks have certain things in common. Many of their ancestors came from central Asia, finally settling in **Anatolia**.

The early Turks lived alongside Armenians, Greeks, Kurds, and Arabs. Over the centuries, various tribes settled in what is now Turkey. Today, Turkey's people have mixed heritage. Some Turks have olive skin, dark hair, and brown eyes. Others are fair-skinned with blond hair and blue eyes. Perhaps Turkey's founder Atatürk said it best. He noted, *"Biz bize benzeriz,"* or in English, "We resemble ourselves."[1]

About three out of four people belong to the Turkish ethnic group. They speak the country's official language, Turkish. Another 18 percent of Turkey's people are Kurdish. The Kurds are a Middle Eastern ethnic group. They lived for thousands of years in a region called Kurdistan. Today most Kurds live in eastern Turkey and speak Kurdish. Other ethnic groups include Greeks, Arabs, Armenians, and Jews.

Almost everyone (99.8 percent) in Turkey is Muslim.[2] Muslims follow the teachings and practices of Islam. Islam is a religion which has only one God, Allah. The Quran is the holy book for Muslims. Friday is Islam's holiest day of the week. Islam is divided into two major groups, Sunni (SOON-nee) and Shia (SHEE-uh). Most Turks are Sunni Muslims.

The Five Pillars of Islam are duties that are required of all Muslims. First, Muslims must state that, "there is no god but

Allah and Muhammad is his **prophet**." Muslims believe that Muhammad was chosen to spread Allah's message to the world. He was the founder of Islam.

The second pillar is daily prayer. Muslims must pray five times a day. Before praying, Muslims wash their hands, arms, feet, and face. They then face the holy city of Mecca while praying. Men are required to pray in the mosque whenever possible, but women are not obligated to do the same. However, women *are* allowed to pray at the mosque. They usually sit separately from male worshippers.

The third pillar involves fasting. Muslims can choose to fast on certain days, but during the holy month of Ramadan fasting is required for healthy adults. Throughout Ramadan, the faithful don't eat or drink from before sunrise until after sundown.

Islam's fourth pillar is giving to the poor. Muslims must give away a certain percentage of their wealth each year. They may give money directly to people in need, or they can donate through their mosque.

The last pillar is the *Hajj*. The Hajj is a religious journey to Mecca, the Muslim holy city. Muslims must go on this pilgrimage at least once during their lifetime. People who can't afford to go or are not healthy enough to travel are not required to perform the Hajj, however.

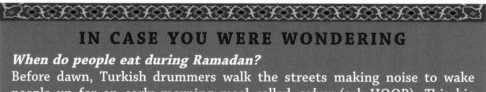

IN CASE YOU WERE WONDERING

When do people eat during Ramadan?
Before dawn, Turkish drummers walk the streets making noise to wake people up for an early morning meal called *sahur* (sah-HOOR). This big breakfast helps Muslims get through the fast. At the end of the day's fast, people enjoy a meal called *iftar* (eef-TAHR). Turks feast on cheeses, olives, dates, pide bread, meats, vegetables, and fruits.

A Turkish woman
reading from the
Quran

Muslims share certain values. Many of these values come from the Quran. For example, Muslims are taught to respect their parents. They strive to perform good deeds and help others.

Millions of Turkish Muslims are Alevis. The Alevis believe in one God and that Muhammad was a prophet. However, the Alevi faith also includes beliefs from other religions. Some of their traditions come from Arab faiths that existed before Muhammad's time. Like Sufi Muslims, Alevis believe that the Quran has hidden meanings. Most Alevi beliefs are passed down by oral tradition, though. The Alevis live mainly in east and southeastern Anatolia.

Gender roles are important in Turkey. Under Turkish law, women and men have equal rights. Women can study at universities. They can choose interesting careers. Women working outside the home are more common in the cities than in the countryside. In 1993, Tansu Çiller became Turkey's first female prime minister. It marked a step in the right direction for Turkish women's rights.

Despite the fact that Turkish law treats men and women as equals, many Turkish families maintain traditional gender roles. Some still believe that a son's birth is more important than a daughter's birth. Rural women are less likely to appear in public on their own. In some cases, husbands make most of the decisions because their wives have been taught to be obedient to men. But today's Turks are incorporating new values with traditional ones. These values can vary greatly from one region to another, and from one family to another. As Turkey continues to modernize, it will be interesting to see the changes in men's and women's roles.

ISLAMIC EXTREMISTS

Car bombs exploding on a crowded street. Neighborhoods destroyed. You may have heard the term "terrorism" before. What does it mean? And why do some people commit such violent acts? Terrorists try to frighten others or use violence in order to get what they want. They believe in many different causes and have caused damage and deaths around the world.

Because some of these terrorists call themselves Muslims, there are people who may be afraid of all Muslims. But terrorists with extreme views are not like most Muslims. Al-Qaeda and Hezbollah are examples of extremist Islamic groups. In 2001, al-Qaeda members crashed planes into New York City's Twin Towers. Al-Qaeda believed that the United States was helping their enemies, and decided to declare a "holy war." It can be hard to understand why extremists do the things they do. Such violent acts do not make sense to most people.

It is important to understand that most Muslims are just like most Christians, Jews, or Buddhists in many ways. They are good. They are faithful. They help less fortunate people. Muslims have families and they celebrate holidays with their families and friends. They pray at their local mosque. Most Muslims in Turkey and around the globe go about their daily business just like you without harming other people. Most Muslims are also tolerant of other people who don't share their religious beliefs.

Similar to many people around the world, Muslims in Turkey and other Middle Eastern countries work, pray, and enjoy a variety of activities.

Turkish singer
Tarkan performs
live during a
concert in
Hamburg,
Germany.

CHAPTER 4
Culture in Turkey

Art. Music. Literature. Turkey has a rich cultural heritage. Many cultural traditions exist throughout Turkey in a fascinating blend of East and West.

Music and dance are important parts of Turkish culture. Traditional music includes folk, classical, and Ottoman military music. Some Westerners describe Turkish music as "flat" or "off-key." Why? Classical Turkish music uses sounds that are very different from what we're used to hearing.

Turkish musicians play a variety of instruments. Many are unknown to others around the world. Folk musicians in Turkey play the *saz*, a stringed instrument with three strings and a long neck. In eastern Turkey, people play the *tulum*, an instrument that is like a bagpipe.

In the past, Ottoman military music was played as troops went into battle. These bands played cymbals, oboes, and drums quite loudly. The music was intended to give troops courage as they fought. It was also a sign of the power and majesty of the Ottoman Empire.

Just like in Europe or in America, Turks might turn on the radio and hear pop music. Turkish pop music is a unique blend of Western and Eastern sounds. It often has a **techno** beat. Two popular musicians in Turkey are Tarkan Tevetoğlu and Sezen Aksu. Tarkan is known as the "Prince of Pop," while people call Sezen the "Queen of Turkish Pop."

Saz

Have you heard of belly dancing? Turkish belly dancers perform to folk music known as *çiftetelli*. This music features violins and cymbals and is quite energetic. Belly dancers frequently perform at weddings or parties.

Members of an Islamic sect called the Mevlevi have a creative music and dance tradition. The Mevlevi are sometimes called Whirling Dervishes. They dance to soothing, mystical music. Each December in the city of Konya, the Mevlana Festival showcases this incredible dancing. Dancers wear long, flowing white gowns and tall hats and whirl to the beat of the music. The Mevlevi see this dancing as a way of becoming closer to Allah. They play traditional Turkish instruments, including the *kudüm*—a pair of small drums, and the *ney*—a wooden flute.

People in Turkey like to go to the movies. Some of the films they watch are from the United States and other countries. But

Whirling
Dervishes

Turkish directors also make their own films with Turkish actors. These movies often focus on the recent changes in Turkish society.

Turks enjoy reading many types of literature. Aziz Nesin (1915–1995) was one of Turkey's most popular writers. His short stories and novels still appeal to readers today. Nâzim Hikmet (1902–1963) was a Turkish poet. Hikmet's poems showed his love of his country as well as his criticisms of his homeland. Hikmet spent many years in jail for speaking out about his beliefs. Orhan Pamuk is a famous Turkish writer. His novels are often about life in modern Turkey. In 2006, Pamuk won the Nobel Prize in Literature. He continues to write today.

Turkish artisans are well-known for their beautiful handicrafts. They have made carpets, baskets, wood and stone carvings, and embroidered fabrics for centuries. Craftspeople also create lamps, pots, and decorative objects from brass or copper. Both tourists and locals buy artwork and handicrafts from Turkey's many markets.

People celebrate Turkey's beautiful ceramic art. Turkish bowls and tiles come in many rich colors. Artists often use floral designs or geometric patterns in their art. Detailed ceramic tiles

Traditional Ottoman ceramic

often decorate Turkish mosques. Many international visitors come to see the incredible floral tiles in Istanbul's Topkapi Palace.

Shadow-puppet theater is a traditional part of Turkish culture. It began hundreds of years ago when the Ottoman Empire ruled the land of Turkey. Shadow puppets can represent people or animals. They are often made out of leather, then painted or stained. How do shadow puppets work? A lamp is placed behind a white screen, and the puppets create shadows on the screen. Sticks attached to the backs of the puppets allow the puppeteers to move them. The screen is very thin, so the details and colors of the puppets can shine through clearly. Karagöz is a popular character in Turkish shadow-puppet shows. Karagöz is hunched over and wears brightly colored traditional clothing. Karagöz and his friend Hacivat often get themselves into silly situations. Shadow-puppet shows entertain Turkish children and adults. They can still be seen at performance halls and museums throughout the country.

Hacivat

Karagöz

Turkey is a food lover's paradise. From special occasion foods to everyday meals, Turks take pride in their cooking. Turkish families eat most meals together at home. For breakfast, people normally eat bread with honey, jam, or butter. Breakfast can also include olives, feta cheese, tomatoes, and cucumbers. Eggs are popular as well. Most Turks start their day with a cup of tea.

Rice, soup, or pasta are regular lunch options. City dwellers may eat lunch at a *lokanta* (loh-KAHN-tuh), a basic Turkish restaurant. The food here is usually already prepared. Like a school cafeteria, diners choose the dishes they want and pay.[1] These restaurants offer soup, rice dishes, meats, and stews. The

Turkish
Delight

IN CASE YOU WERE WONDERING

What treats are popular in Turkey?
From pastries to candies, Turks love sweets. One of the most popular desserts is baklava, a pastry layered with honey and nuts. Puddings such as rice pudding are common, too. To Americans, the pudding called *aşure* might seem unusual. What's in it? Everyone makes it a little differently, but it often contains beans, rice, chickpeas, nuts, sugar, and dried fruits. Have you ever heard of Turkish Delight? Turks call this candy *lokum*. It's a jelly-like candy coated in powdered sugar. It comes in many flavors, including lemon, rose, pistachio, and hazelnut.

With its warm, clear air and breathtaking views, Turkey's Mugla Province offers some of the best paragliding in the world.

stews often contain meat (chicken, lamb, fish, or beef) and vegetables (especially eggplant).

Dinner is the biggest meal of the day in Turkey. Before the meal, people eat appetizers, or *meze*. These may be hot or cold. Common meze are salads and stuffed pastries.[4]

Not everyone in Turkey eats the same foods. The **cuisine** varies among regions and ethnic groups. Families in the central and western regions generally eat lots of soups, wheat, beans, and stewed meat. Turks living near the Black Sea are more likely to eat anchovies or locally grown walnuts. Folks in southeastern Turkey eat foods similar to the foods eaten by their Arab neighbors. They might eat chickpeas, lentils, or spicy **kebabs**.

SHOPPING IN TURKEY

Clothes shopping. Spice shopping. Window shopping. Just like in other parts of the world, people in Turkey shop for two reasons. One is that they need things. The other is for entertainment. Do you ever go to the mall with your friends? Teenagers in Turkey's major cities enjoy going to the mall when they have a day off. Turkish teens enjoy window shopping, checking out the latest styles, or grabbing a snack at the mall's food court. Istanbul's Cevahir Shopping Center is home to about 230 shops on six floors.[5] Sounds like something you might see in New York or Chicago, right?

Many Turks shop at street markets, whether for food items or new outfits. People often bargain at these markets because the prices are not fixed. The vendors are willing to **negotiate** on their prices. Istanbul's Grand Bazaar is one of the largest—and oldest—shopping districts in the world. It was constructed in the fifteenth century. This shopping district is spread out over more than sixty streets.[6] It's larger than seven football fields! The Grand Bazaar has "neighborhoods" for jewelry, clothing, antiques, souvenirs, carpets, and more. When it's time to pray, there's even a mosque. Each day over 250,000 people browse the shops here. With over three thousand shops, Grand Bazaar visitors could truly "shop 'til they drop!"

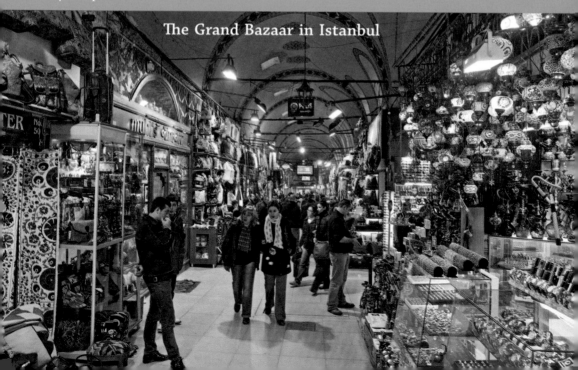

The Grand Bazaar in Istanbul

Stone carving depicting the god Sharruma holding Hittite King Tudhalya in his left arm, Tudhalya's head resting at Sharruma's shoulder. (Sharruma's name means "king of the mountains.") Just a couple of kilometers from the Hittite capital, Hattusa, was the rock sanctuary of Yazilikaya. In addition to the king, about ninety gods and goddesses were carved into the limestone rocks here. These carvings also show animals and mythical beings. The carvings of Yazilikaya, located in central Turkey, are dated from the thirteenth century BCE.

CHAPTER 5
History and Government

Turkey is a land with a rich past. Its history is full of amazing adventures and civilizations. Turkey's location at the intersection of Asia and Europe appealed to many people over time. Numerous trading routes went through this area. Also, much of Turkey's land is good for growing crops. Unfortunately, Turkey's history was not always peaceful. In the Middle East, conflict was common as rulers fought for control of land. For thousands of years, the land that is in present-day Turkey was the site of many of those battles. The fighting was bad. But modern Turkey was also shaped by the cultures of the various peoples who ruled and lived in this land.

Central Turkey was home to some of the world's earliest settlements. About 9,400 years ago, people built Çatalhöyük (CHAHT-uhl-hoo-YOOK), an early agricultural settlement. Archaeologists estimate that thousands of people lived here in mud-brick houses. Some buildings were decorated with murals. People lived in Çatalhöyük for more than two thousand years.[1]

Almost four thousand years ago, the Hittites founded one of Turkey's most important civilizations. It included much of modern-day Turkey, as well as parts of Syria. Hattusa was the Hittite capital. It was a huge city, located a little more than one hundred miles west of present-day Ankara. The Hittites were an advanced civilization. They built incredible temples, created works of art, and made beautiful gold jewelry and pottery. The Hittites also had a professional army to protect their kingdom.

Even with their advanced army, the Hittite Empire had disappeared by about 1190 BCE. No one is sure why this happened. But historical records state that around this time the "Sea Peoples" were raiding towns in the region. Sailing in from the Mediterranean Sea, they attacked many empires along the coast. These raids surely weakened the Hittite Empire, and could have caused its eventual collapse.

Many groups ruled Anatolia after the Hittites, including the Phrygians and the Lydians. Alexander the Great, an important Greek leader, conquered Anatolia in 334 BCE. Greeks began to settle in the region and interacted regularly with the people already living there. The two cultures changed and influenced one another. After Alexander's death, various leaders invaded Anatolia. They came from both east and west, each hoping to rule this land.

Around 130 BCE, Anatolia became a Roman province called Asia. In 330 CE, Emperor Constantine made Byzantium the capital of the Roman Empire and renamed the city Constantinople. The eastern part of the Roman Empire, including Constantinople, grew stronger. The Western Roman Empire was conquered in the late fifth century. But in the East, Anatolia remained under the control of the Roman Empire.

As different people arrived in Anatolia, they brought different religions with them. After the death of Jesus, Christianity spread in the area. It became even more popular in the fourth century CE, when Emperor Constantine became a Christian. But over one thousand miles south of Constantinople, another new religion soon developed. Around 610 CE, a man named Muhammad began receiving messages from the angel Gabriel. The angel brought messages from God, and Muhammad's job was to share these messages with the world. This was the beginning of Islam. After Muhammad's death, his followers continued to spread his message. They also conquered nearby lands, expanding their empires.

This mosaic, which depicts Emperor Constantine, became part of the decoration in Hagia Sophia around 1000 CE.

Most of Anatolia remained part of the Roman Empire in the eighth century CE. Still, Muslims tried to take control of the region many times. Other Muslims traveled to the area peacefully. Over the next couple of centuries, many residents of Anatolia became Muslims themselves.

The Seljuks were Muslim nomads who came to Anatolia from central Asia. They established their own empire during the eleventh century. Their empire included much of modern-day Turkey, which was won in battles with the Romans. The Seljuks introduced the Turkish language to the people here. But when the Seljuk leaders began fighting with each other, their empire began to crumble. The former empire broke into different states. At the same time, Christian armies called Crusaders arrived from Europe. The Crusaders captured Constantinople in 1204 and took control of eastern Anatolia. In western Anatolia, Mongols from Asia finally defeated the remaining Seljuks in the middle of the thirteenth century.

Though many rulers had come and gone, the next empire would last for hundreds of years. The Ottoman Empire was

IN CASE YOU WERE WONDERING

Do all Turks have to serve in the military?
According to the Turkish **constitution**, every healthy male citizen must serve his country. Men are required to register for military service at age twenty. If they are enrolled at a university, they may wait until they've finished their education. Men who haven't attended a university serve longer than university graduates. Men who didn't go to college must serve for twelve months. University-educated men serve for six to twelve months.

In 2011, a new law was passed. This law allows some Turkish men to pay money instead of doing military service. Only certain people qualify for this exception, including Turkish men aged thirty and over, and those who have been working outside the country for at least three years.[2] Men with certain medical conditions are exempt from military duty, and women are not required to register for military service. Turkish women can serve in the military, but only as officers.[3]

central to Turkish history. At its height, the Ottomans controlled Anatolia, the Middle East (from the borders of Iran to Algeria), parts of North Africa, and large areas of Eastern Europe. In 1453, the Ottomans took over Constantinople and renamed the city Istanbul. This new name meant "city of Islam." Istanbul served as the Ottoman Empire's capital for centuries. Art, **architecture**, and literature blossomed during the Ottoman Empire. Education was celebrated. Many ethnic groups and religions lived peacefully within the empire's borders, even though Islam was the official religion of the state. The Ottoman Empire's rule came to an end after World War I (1914–1918).

During World War I, the German-led Central Powers fought against the Allied Powers (including France, the United States, the British Empire, and Russia). The Ottoman Empire fought along with the Central Powers. After the Central Powers were

Construction of present-day Hagia Sophia began in 532 CE. This building was used as a church by Orthodox Christians for over nine hundred years. In 1453, the Ottoman Turks conquered Constantinople. This beautiful cathedral made a strong impression on Ottoman leader Mehmed II. He ordered that Hagia Sophia be converted into a mosque, and it served as one for nearly five centuries. In 1935, Turkish president Atatürk (and his Council of Ministers) converted the building into a museum. This museum continues to attract and impress visitors from around the globe.

defeated in 1918, the Allied Powers took control of Ottoman land. Many Turks were unhappy about being ruled by outsiders. A man named Mustafa Kemal planned to stop this occupation. He led an army that fought to create a new independent state. The Turkish War of Independence lasted from 1919 to 1923.

The Republic of Turkey became an independent country in 1923. Mustafa Kemal was its first president. He took the name Atatürk, meaning "Father of the Turks." Atatürk served as president until his death in 1938. He made many important changes to Turkey's government (see sidebar). Many of these changes were positive. But perhaps the best changes are yet to come for this nation.

IN CASE YOU WERE WONDERING

How is Turkey's government structured?

Turkey is a democratic republic. It has a president, a prime minister, a cabinet, and a legislature. In 2014, the people of Turkey voted to elect their president for the first time. Before 2014, the president was elected by parliament. Turkey's president is the head of state, and makes sure that the government works the way the Turkish constitution intended it to. The prime minister actually heads Turkey's government. He or she is also the leader of the political party with the most seats in parliament. The Turkish cabinet is called the Council of Ministers. The cabinet watches over and manages the various governmental departments.

Turkey's parliament is called the Grand National Assembly. It has 550 members. In 2013, seventy-eight of the members were women.[4] The Grand National Assembly makes laws, declares war, and accepts treaties. The Turkish people vote parliament's members into office. People must be eighteen to vote in Turkey.

The Turkish government has three branches, just like the US government. The president, prime minister, and Council of Ministers make up the executive branch. The legislative, or law-making, branch consists of the Grand National Assembly. Several types of courts make up Turkey's judicial branch. The Constitutional Court determines whether laws made by the legislature are allowed by the Turkish constitution. All court cases in Turkey are decided by judges, not juries.[5]

Turkey is made up of eighty-one provinces, each with its own governor. These provinces are further broken down into districts, **municipalities**, and villages.

MUSTAFA KEMAL ATATÜRK

Mustafa Kemal Atatürk was born in 1881 in Salonika, which is in modern-day Greece. His childhood wasn't perfect. Mustafa's father died in 1888. Four of his five siblings did not live to become adults. Mustafa went to military junior and senior high schools and was a bright student. Sometime between 1896 and 1899, Mustafa's math teacher gave him the name Kemal,[6] meaning "the perfect one."[7]

Mustafa continued his military studies. He graduated from Istanbul's Military College in 1902 and the Military Academy in 1905. He held many posts over the next fifteen years or so. Mustafa served as the Chief of Staff of the Army Corps. He fought in battles during the Balkan War and World War I, and was a leader in Turkey's War for Independence (1919–1923).[8]

In 1923, Mustafa Kemal Atatürk founded what is now Turkey and became the country's first president. He made Ankara the capital of the new republic. He believed that government should be kept separate from religion. He replaced Islamic laws with European-style laws. In fact, Turkish laws were based on Swiss, French, and Italian laws.[9]

Mustafa Kemal Atatürk and his wife Latife Uşşaki

Atatürk changed Turkey in many ways. He modernized the country and replaced the Islamic lunar calendar with the Gregorian calendar. Atatürk also changed the way Turks read and wrote. To replace the old Ottoman-Arabic alphabet, he had a new Latin alphabet created, similar to the alphabet that English-speakers use. He hoped that it would help Turks to communicate more easily with people in the West.[10] Atatürk improved Turkish schools. He also advanced women's rights, giving women the right to vote and hold political office. He outlawed polygyny, a practice in which a man has more than one wife.

Air pollution in Istanbul, Turkey

CHAPTER 6
Current Issues in Turkey

Earthquakes. The state of the economy. Political disagreements. Pollution. During the twenty-first century, the Turks will face a number of issues.

Turkey is a land of natural beauty. Unfortunately, it also has some environmental challenges. Turkey is located in one of Earth's most active earthquake zones. The North Anatolian Fault runs through Turkey. Here two **tectonic** plates, the Anatolian Plate and the Eurasian Plate, are sliding past each other. Over a dozen earthquakes have occurred in this part of Turkey in the twentieth century.

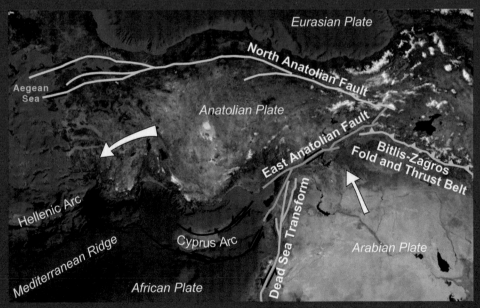

Tectonic plates and faults in Turkey. Most of Turkey lies on the Anatolian plate, which is being squeezed westwards toward the Aegean Sea. Along the North Anatolian Fault, large earthquakes have been occurring, each one further west than the last. Because of this pattern, scientists think that an earthquake could hit Istanbul soon.

IN CASE YOU WERE WONDERING

What happened in the 1999 İzmit earthquake?

One of Turkey's worst earthquakes in recent history took place in 1999 near İzmit. (İzmit is located about fifty-five miles east of Istanbul.) During this quake, the earth shook for over forty-five seconds. It hit in the middle of the night and killed at least seventeen thousand people. Many of these people died when their homes collapsed. In the rapidly growing cities, homes and apartment buildings are built quickly to provide housing for everyone. But they're often not strong enough to stand up to an earthquake. Turkish leaders have promised to make sure more homes are built to resist these earthquakes in the future. For now, however, many people continue to live in homes that could be unsafe in an earthquake.

Another challenge for Turkey is water pollution in the Bosporus Strait. This twenty-mile-long channel is an important aquatic habitat. Dolphins, fish, and a variety of other marine life live here. Each day a huge volume of traffic crosses the Bosporus. Some of this traffic includes giant oil tankers. Ferryboats, fishing boats, and freighters also travel here. Oil spills have occurred in the past, and environmentalists worry that another one could happen soon. Wastewater from the city's residents and boat exhaust can also harm the Bosporus's animals. As the local population and ship traffic continue to increase, it will be important to make changes to improve the Bosporus's water quality. Some people want to build a pipeline to deliver oil across the strait. They hope to take the oil tankers out of the water and lower the risk of a spill. Scientists are also monitoring water pollution in other Turkish bodies of water.

The Turkish economy has struggled in the last few years. Part of the problem is a trade imbalance. Turkey imports more goods from other countries than it exports. In other words, Turkey spent more money buying things from other countries than it earned from selling its own products to other countries.

This can create new jobs in the countries that Turkey buys its goods from. But over time, it also means fewer new jobs are being created in Turkey.

Finding a good job is especially hard for people who have recently moved into Turkish cities. While some Turks live very well, others have trouble putting food on the table. Some

Cargo ship on the Bosporus Strait

IN CASE YOU WERE WONDERING

What products does Turkey buy from other countries?
Like all countries, Turkey does not make everything it needs. It must import, or bring in, some goods from other countries. For example, Turkey does not produce all the energy it needs. It takes a lot of fuel to run the country's cars and machinery. Turkey also needs energy for its factories and homes. So one product Turkey imports is fuel. Turkey also brings in chemicals, machinery, and transportation equipment. Where does Turkey get all these things? Turkey imports from many countries. But its four largest suppliers of goods are Russia, Germany, China, and the United States.[1]

young people leave Turkey, hoping to make a better living. Over five million Turks currently live abroad. About 80 percent of them live in Western European countries.[2]

How do poor families manage? Sometimes the children work. Rural children commonly work in the fields during the day. Some primary schools in the countryside have two shifts. That way, all the students can attend classes and still work at home. In other cases, kids have jobs in factories. Some help their parents with a family business. Sadly, some children end up living on the streets. They may sell tissues or water bottles to earn money.

Turkey's government also causes disagreements. It is a secular government, and many people want it to stay that way. Like Atatürk, they believe that religion should be a private matter. They don't want religion to control the government. Others want Turkey to become an Islamic state, meaning that Islamic law would become Turkish law. Many countries in the Middle East, including Iran, Iraq, and Saudi Arabia, have Islamic governments.

Since 1946, Turkey has been a democratic republic with many political parties. Since 2002, the Justice and Development Party (AKP) has had the most seats in parliament. Although this party has clear Islamic roots, the party's leaders have so far chosen to keep Turkey secular. Founded by Atatürk, the Republican People's Party (CHP) is another important political party in Turkey. Many members of this party worry that the Justice and Development Party wants to create Islamic laws in Turkey.

Still, Turkey has strong leaders and creative thinkers. When these people work together to solve the nation's problems, they can ensure a brighter future for everyone.

KURDS

One cannot talk about Turkey's people without discussing the Kurds. The Kurds are the largest **minority** group in Turkey, making up about 18 percent of Turkey's population.[3] For thousands of years, the Kurds lived in Kurdistan. This area was mostly controlled by the Ottoman Empire prior to World War I. When the war ended, the hilly land of Kurdistan was divided among Iran, Iraq, Syria, and Turkey. This was difficult for the Kurds now living in Turkey. The new government expected them to learn Turkish. Many Kurds had to leave their old ways behind and abandon some of their traditional customs.

Some Kurds struggled to fit into Turkish society. The Turkish government banned speaking Kurdish for years. Even now that the ban has been lifted, its effects continue. Many children were taught Turkish at school, but spoke Kurdish at home. They now struggle to learn to read and write their own language. But language was just one source of tension between Kurds and Turks.[4]

The Kurdistan Workers' Party (or PKK) is a Kurdish political party. PKK members have been fighting for decades to get their own independent state. During the 1980s and 1990s, the PKK carried out terrorist acts in hopes of achieving this goal. More recently, though, the PKK has changed its focus. Its members now hope to win more civil rights. Ideally, they want to rule themselves within the country of Turkey.[5]

Most Kurds live in southeastern Turkey, which is the poorest part of the country. Since the 1950s, many Kurds have left the countryside. Some went to Istanbul, which now has the largest population of Kurds of any single Turkish province. Others moved overseas, many to Western European countries. Germany is home to the largest overseas community of Turkish Kurds.[6]

Kurdish soldiers stand guard in Arbil, Iraq (also part of Kurdistan).

The Atatürk Dam is located on the Euphrates River in southeastern Turkey. This dam is the largest in a series of twenty-two dams on both the Tigris and Euphrates Rivers that are part of the Southeastern Anatolian Project. Construction began on this dam in 1983 and was completed in 1990. It was built to both provide irrigation water and hydroelectricity to arid southeastern Turkey.

CHAPTER 7
Turkey in the Global Community

Throughout its history, Turkey has been part of the global community. In the past, traders passed through on their Silk Road journeys. Today, tourists arrive by jet for their vacations. Turkey still hosts all kinds of people. Turkey has high-tech communication and transportation systems which allow Turkey to trade and share ideas with the rest of the world.

Water is one of Turkey's most valuable resources. Turkey is fortunate to have many rivers, including the Tigris and Euphrates Rivers. Throughout the Middle East, people have fought over access to water for thousands of years. Everyone wants their fair share of this life-giving liquid. The Turkish government is working on a huge development project called GAP, or the Southeastern Anatolian Project. As part of this project, Turkey is building twenty-two dams and nineteen **hydroelectric** power plants on the Tigris and Euphrates Rivers. Construction is planned for completion by 2015. The new dams will provide water to areas that would otherwise be too dry to farm, while the hydroelectric power plants will create electricity from the dams. Experts estimate that these power plants could provide up to 25 percent of Turkey's electricity.

Turkey's economy is important to the world. The country exports many goods to other countries. Turkey is the world's leading producer of hazelnuts, apricots, and cherries. It exports many of its agricultural products to the European Union (EU) and the United States. Turkey's automotive, electronics, and construction industries are also growing. Turkey also imports products that it needs from other nations. Germany, Russia, and Iran are three of Turkey's major trading partners.[1]

Turkey has been part of the global community in many positive ways. Turkey joined the North Atlantic Treaty Organization (or NATO) in 1952. The purpose of NATO is to ensure the freedom and security of its members. It works to promote democratic values. NATO members try to resolve conflicts peacefully whenever possible. Today NATO has twenty-eight member countries including the United States, Canada, the United Kingdom, Italy, and France.

Since 2011, civil war has been a part of life in Syria. Thousands of Syrian citizens joined together and began fighting against their government. Innocent people have died in this fight, including small children. Hoping to protect their families, millions of Syrian people have left the country. Since Turkey and Syria share a 511-mile (822-kilometer) border, many of these people fled to Turkey. By October 2013, over six hundred

In March 2012, children in Istanbul, Turkey, participated in a demonstration protesting the violence that the Syrian government had been using against its citizens.

thousand Syrian **refugees** were living in Turkey.[2] Some live in refugee camps near the border. Others rent homes or rooms outside these camps. Turkey has spent billions of dollars providing camps for the refugees. Still, the government leaders say they will continue to help these people.

Not all of Turkey's international relationships have been easy. Cyprus is an island located south of Turkey in the Mediterranean Sea. It was a British colony until it won its independence in 1960. Both Greeks and Turks live on Cyprus, and each group has its own culture and language. These groups fought for control of the island for decades. Some of these conflicts involved military force. In 1983, the Turkish-occupied part of Cyprus declared itself independent, and called itself the Turkish Republic of Northern Cyprus. Only Turkey recognizes this self-declared state. Talks between Greek and Turkish **Cypriots** are ongoing.

IN CASE YOU WERE WONDERING

Why isn't Turkey a member of the EU?
Turkey wants to become a member of the European Union (or EU). The country first applied for membership in 1987. The EU is an economic and political partnership consisting of twenty-eight European countries. These nations share a common currency, the euro, and work together on issues. EU members try to solve environmental problems. EU residents can travel and work freely throughout much of Europe. The EU also promotes human rights. EU members must provide all their citizens with freedom, human dignity, and equality.

Turkey and the EU have had some disagreements. The EU hasn't been satisfied with some of Turkey's human rights policies. For example, Turkish law limits freedom of speech.[3] In 2013, people across Turkey participated in a protest against the government. When riot police intervened, over eight thousand people were injured. Dozens of people were detained.[4] Another issue is that Turkey hasn't opened its ports and airports to Cypriot planes and boats. Finally, Turkey and the EU don't see eye-to-eye about Cyprus's status as an independent nation. While negotiations about these issues continue, Turkey is officially a European Union candidate country.

In November 2013, Greek Cypriot students demonstrate against the thirty-year anniversary of the proclamation of the Turkish Republic of Northern Cyprus. These students in Nicosia, Cyprus, are waving both Greek and Cypriot flags.

Turkey has a unique position in the global community. The country's blend of Islam and democracy appeals to allies around the globe. Economically, culturally, and politically, Turkey has much to offer the world. And with new changes taking place every day, it looks like Turkey may become even more of a global leader in the future.

IN CASE YOU WERE WONDERING

Does the United States have a good relationship with Turkey?
Turkey and the United States have been political and military allies for over fifty years. The two countries share many goals. Both want a more stable Middle East. Both are working to stop terrorism. Turkey and the United States are also active trading partners.

Of course, the United States and Turkey do disagree on some issues. For example, in 2003, the United States wanted to cross Turkish land to invade Iraq. Turkey said no.[5] The United States also believes that Turkey's military is more involved in politics than it should be as a democratic nation. Despite these differences, it seems likely that Turkey and the United States will be economic and political partners for the foreseeable future.

TOURISM IN TURKEY

Turkey is a land of beauty. It has rich history and culture. All these things appeal to tourists from around the world. Vacationers flock to the beaches on the Mediterranean, Aegean, and Black Seas. Sports fans enjoy skiing and snowboarding during the winter. Turkey's scenic areas, like Cappadocia and Pamukkale, are also popular with tourists. Cappadocia, located in central Turkey, has very unusual rock formations. It was a center of early Christianity. Visitors today can see many old churches built out of the area's volcanic rock. Pamukkale is an area with huge cliffs and hot springs. In Turkish, *Pamukkale* means "cotton castle." White "terraces" were formed here when water flowing from the springs left minerals behind. They look as though they're covered in snow.

In Cappadocia tourists can take hot air balloon rides over the rock formations.

History lovers enjoy vacationing in Turkey. Budding archaeologists can see the famous ruins of Troy or Hieropolis. Turkey also has amazing architecture. Tourists visit the courtyards, gardens, and library of Topkapi Palace. Others admire Hagia Sophia, known as the "Church of Holy Wisdom." Its domes, minarets, and artwork are dazzling. Some tourists take Turkish cooking classes. Others tour Istanbul's spice markets or its Grand Bazaar.

Whether Americans are visiting Ankara or Turks are traveling to Thrace, there is no shortage of things to do in Turkey.

MENEMEN

Menemen is a classic Turkish dish. It consists of eggs, peppers, onions, and tomatoes. Turkish cooks usually add spices such as salt, pepper, and oregano. Some add hot chili peppers or olives, too. Turks enjoy menemen as a breakfast dish, but it can make a great lunch or dinner. It's also a popular street food. Be sure to have **an adult** help you with this, since there is chopping and hot oil involved. This recipe makes enough for four people.

Ingredients

½ cup olive oil
1 onion, sliced
1 red or green
   pepper, seeds
   taken out and
   chopped
2 large tomatoes,
   peeled and diced
4 eggs
salt and pepper

Instructions

1. Whisk the eggs lightly, and add salt and pepper.
2. Heat the olive oil in a heavy frying pan. Stir in chopped pepper and onions. Cook for 3–6 minutes until they start to soften, but aren't brown.
3. Add the tomatoes to the pan, mixing well. Cook for 5–7 minutes more, until the liquid has reduced a bit.
4. Stir in the eggs. Continue to stir as it cooks for another 1–2 minutes, until firm.

EBRU (MARBLED PAPER)

Marbled paper is known as *ebru* in Turkish. For centuries, ebru has been a traditional art form in Turkey. The Topkapi Palace has an example of marbling on display that dates back to 1447. It was widely used in the binding of books. In fact, book lovers in Europe prized ebru. They often referred to it as "Turkish papers." Another common use of ebru was within calligraphic panels. In its early days, artists even created ebru for government documents.

Traditionally, when Turkish artists created ebru, they used a number of materials that are not easily available in the United States. For example, they used a plant gum called tragacanth to thicken the water before painting. And the traditional clay paint was mixed with ox bile (a digestive fluid). This version of paper marbling uses easy-to-find materials that most people already have at home.

Materials

Several sheets of plain white paper
Several colors of food coloring
9x13 aluminum foil pan
Newspaper or a cloth

A can of white foam shaving cream
A few toothpicks
A thin piece of cardboard or plastic
(such as a ruler)

Instructions

1. Cover the surface that you want to work on with either newspaper or a large cloth. This will prevent any messes and make your cleanup easy.
2. Cover the foil pan with a layer of shaving cream.
3. Choose the shades of food coloring you want to use. Drip the food coloring, a little at a time, on top of the shaving cream. It is best to use only a little food coloring so the colors don't run together too much.
4. Take a toothpick and gently run it through the shaving cream on the pan. The idea is to create swirls of color.
5. Place a sheet of clean white paper on top of the swirly shaving cream. Rub your hand gently over the paper, making sure that the shaving cream has coated all of the paper.
6. Remove the paper from the pan. Use a thin piece of cardboard or plastic to wipe the thick shaving cream from the paper. You should see the marbled design on your paper.
7. Allow your paper to dry thoroughly. If it curls, you can use a book to keep it flat. Hang the paper up to display your ebru!

WHAT YOU SHOULD KNOW ABOUT TURKEY

Official Name: Republic of Turkey

Official Language: Turkish

Population: 80,694,485 (July 2013 estimate)

Land Area: 297,157 square miles (769,632 square kilometers)

Coastline: 4,474 miles (7,200 kilometers)

Bordering Countries: Armenia, Azerbaijan, Bulgaria, Georgia, Greece, Iran, Iraq, Syria

Capital City: Ankara

Government Type: Republican parliamentary democracy

Other Major Cities: Istanbul, İzmir, Bursa, Adana

Ethnic Groups: Turkish 70-75%, Kurdish 18%, other minorities 7-12%

Religions: Muslim 99.8%, other—mostly Christians and Jews 0.2%

Literacy Rate: 94.1% (97.9% male, 90.3% female)

Highest Point: Mount Ararat—16,949 feet (5,166 meters)

Currency: Turkish lira

Important Holidays: National Sovereignty and Children's Day (April 23), Victory Day (August 30), Republic Day (October 29)

Famous Landmarks: Topkapi Palace, Blue Mosque, Grand Bazaar, Hagia Sophia (Istanbul); Cappadocia (Central Anatolia)

Flag: A red background featuring a white crescent moon and star, the design of modern-day Turkey's flag is similar to the banner of the Ottoman Empire. The crescent moon and star are also traditional symbols of Islam. According to legend, the flag represents the moon and star's reflection in a pool of blood of Turkish warriors.

TIMELINE

BCE

ca. 7400	An early agricultural settlement is founded at Çatalhöyük.
ca. 1600–1200	The Hittite Empire thrives in Anatolia.
334	Alexander the Great conquers Anatolia.
ca. 130	Anatolia becomes the Roman province "Asia."

CE

330	The Roman Emperor Constantine makes Byzantium his capital and renames the city Constantinople.
ca. 610	The prophet Muhammad begins receiving messages from the angel Gabriel, marking the beginning of Islam.
ca. 1040–1157	The Seljuk empire thrives in the Middle East, including much of modern-day Turkey.
1204	Constantinople is captured by Christian Crusaders.
1243	Mongols take control of western Anatolia.
1453	Ottoman forces conquer Constantinople, the Byzantine capital, and they rename the city Istanbul. Istanbul University is founded.
1609	Construction of the Blue Mosque begins.
1918	The Ottoman Empire is defeated in World War I.
1919–1923	The Turkish War of Independence.
1923	The Republic of Turkey is established; Mustafa Kemal becomes president.
1928	Turkey becomes secular; the clause keeping Islam as state religion is removed from Turkey's constitution.
1934	Turkish women are allowed to vote and be elected to office for the first time.
1938	Mustafa Kemal Atatürk dies.
1945	During World War II, Turkey declares war on Japan and Germany. Turkey joins the United Nations.
1950	Turkey holds its first free general election with multiple parties.
1952	Turkey joins NATO, the North Atlantic Treaty Organization.
1960	The army takes over the government, beginning a period of military rule.
1974	Turkish troops invade northern Cyprus.
1976	An earthquake in the Van province kills about five thousand people.
1980	Martial law (military government) is extended after civil unrest.
1982	Turkey's new constitution changes parliament to a single house.
1983	The Turkish Republic of Northern Cyprus is established.
1987	Turkey applies for membership in the European Union (EU).
1990	Turkey allows United Nations forces to launch air strikes against Iraq from Turkish bases.
1993	Tansu Çiller becomes the first female prime minister of Turkey.
1995	Turkish troops launch a military offensive against Kurds in northern Iraq.
1999	The İzmit earthquake along the North Anatolian Fault kills over seventeen thousand people.
2002	The Islamic Justice and Development Party (AKP) wins a majority in the election, but promises to keep Turkey's laws secular. Turkish men are no longer considered head of family by law; women are now officially equal with men under Turkish law.
2004	Turkey bans the death penalty under all circumstances.
2006	Turkish writer Orhan Pamuk wins the Nobel Prize in Literature.
2011	The ban on headscarves at universities is lifted. Certain men are now allowed to pay money instead of serving in the military.
2012	Turkey allows schools to offer Kurdish language as optional course.
2013	The ban on headscarves for female workers in state offices is lifted. Anti-government protests are held in cities across Turkey; police respond with violence. A rail line is opened under the Bosporus Strait, connecting Asia and Europe.
2014	The length of mandatory military service for non-university graduates is reduced from fifteen months to twelve months. The first election is planned for August 10, which allows Turks to elect their president directly.

CHAPTER NOTES

Chapter 1. Welcome to Turkey!

1. Cengiz and Heather Cigeroglu, interview with the author, November 2, 2013.

2. Tristan Rutherford and Kathryn Tomasetti, *Istanbul & Western Turkey* (Washington, DC: National Geographic Society, 2011), p. 43.

3. Suzanne Swan, *Turkey* (London: DK Publishing, 2003), p. 341.

Chapter 2. City and Country Life in Turkey

1. CIA, *The World Factbook*, "Turkey," January 14, 2014. https://www.cia.gov/library/publications/the-world-factbook/geos/tu.html

2. Dana Facaros and Michael Pauls, *Turkey* (Northampton, MA: Cadogan Guides USA, 2009), p. 98.

3. Aysu Kes-Erkul, *International Journal of Humanities and Social Science*, "Neighborhood Effects and Reproduction of Poverty: A Social Housing Case from Turkey," vol. 3, no. 20, December 2013. http://www.ijhssnet.com/journals/Vol_3_No_20_December_2013/15.pdf

Chapter 3. The People of Turkey

1. Robert P. Finn, *Light Millennium*, "Ataturk's World View," Fall 2010. http://www.lightmillennium.org/2010_24th/robert_p_finn_ataturk_world_view.html

2. CIA, *The World Factbook*, "Turkey," January 14, 2014. https://www.cia.gov/library/publications/the-world-factbook/geos/tu.html

3. Blue Mosque, "History." http://www.bluemosque.co/history.html

4. Tristan Rutherford and Kathryn Tomasetti, *Istanbul & Western Turkey* (Washington, DC: National Geographic Society, 2011), p. 71.

Chapter 4. Culture in Turkey

1. Suzanne Swan, *Turkey* (London: DK Publishing, 2003), p. 336.

2. *Today's Zaman*, "40 Percent of Turks Never Go on Holiday," September 8, 2008. http://www.todayszaman.com/newsDetail_getNewsById.action;jsessionid=496ECC2A1DD77BFCB8D185EB9ACB5D0B?newsId=152470

3. Ibid.

4. Dana Facaros and Michael Pauls, *Turkey* (Northampton, MA: Cadogan Guides USA, 2009), pp. 52–55.

5. Istanbul Cevahir, "About Us." http://www.istanbulcevahir.com/en-EN/about-us/46.aspx

6. Tristan Rutherford and Kathryn Tomasetti, *Istanbul & Western Turkey* (Washington, DC: National Geographic Society, 2011), pp. 79–81.

Chapter 5. History and Brief Government Overview

1. UNESCO, "Neolithic Site of Çatalhöyük." http://whc.unesco.org/en/list/1405

2. Joe Parkinson, *Wall Street Journal*, "Turkey Unveils Changes to Military Obligations," November 24, 2011. http://online.wsj.com/news/articles/SB10001424052970204443404577054432267092986

3. CIA, *The World Factbook*, "Turkey," January 14, 2014. https://www.cia.gov/library/publications/the-world-factbook/geos/tu.html

CHAPTER NOTES

4. Quota Project, "Grand National Assembly in Turkey," July 1, 2013. http://www.quotaproject.org/uid/countryview.cfm?country=223

5. Law Society of England and Wales, "Turkey." http://international.lawsociety.org.uk/ip/europe/582/profile

6. Republic Of Turkey: Ministry Of Culture And Tourism, "Biography of Atatürk." http://www.kultur.gov.tr/EN,31350/biography-of-ataturk.html

7. Ohio State University Department of History, "Mustafa Kemal Ataturk." http://ehistory.osu.edu/world/PeopleView.cfm?PID=213

8. Ibid.

9. Sibel Bozdoğan and Reşat Kasaba, eds., *Rethinking Modernity and National Identity in Turkey* (Seattle, WA: University of Washington Press, 1997), p. 71.

10. Banu Eligür, *The Mobilization of Political Islam in Turkey* (New York: Cambridge University Press, 2010), p. 43.

Chapter 6. Current Issues In Turkey Today

1. CIA, *The World Factbook*, "Turkey," January 14, 2014. https://www.cia.gov/library/publications/the-world-factbook/geos/tu.html

2. Republic of Turkey Ministry of Foreign Affairs, "Turkish Citizens Living Abroad." http://www.mfa.gov.tr/the-expatriate-turkish-citizens.en.mfa

3. CIA, *The World Factbook*, "Turkey," January 14, 2014. https://www.cia.gov/library/publications/the-world-factbook/geos/tu.html

4. Başak İnce, *Citizenship and Identity in Turkey* (London: I.B. Tauris & Co Ltd, 2012), p. 55.

5. Greg Bruno, Council on Foreign Relations, "Inside the Kurdistan Workers Party (PKK)," October 19, 2007. http://www.cfr.org/turkey/inside-kurdistan-workers-party-pkk/p14576

6. Bill Park, *Modern Turkey* (New York: Routledge, 2012), p. 92.

Chapter 7. Turkey as Part of the Global Community

1. CIA, *The World Factbook*, "Turkey," January 14, 2014. https://www.cia.gov/library/publications/the-world-factbook/geos/tu.html

2. Humeyra Pamuk, Reuters, "Number of Syrian Refugees in Turkey Exceeds 600,000: Turkish Official," October 21, 2013. http://www.reuters.com/article/2013/10/21/us-syria-crisis-turkey-refugees-idUSBRE99K04O20131021

3. Stephen Kinzer, *Reset: Iran, Turkey, and America's Future* (New York: Times Books, 2010), p. 199.

4. Sebnem Arsu, *New York Times*, "Turkish Police Detain 30 in Crackdown on Demonstrators," July 16, 2013. http://www.nytimes.com/2013/07/17/world/europe/turkish-crackdown-on-demonstrators.html?_r=1&

5. Stephen Kinzer, *Reset: Iran, Turkey, and America's Future* (New York: Times Books, 2010), p. 198.

FURTHER READING

For Young Readers

Jackson, Elaine. *Discover Turkey*. New York: Powerkids Press, 2011.

Lilly, Alexandra. *Teens in Turkey*. North Mankato, MN: Compass Point Books, 2008.

Owings, Lisa. *Turkey*. Minneapolis, MN: Bellweather Media, Inc., 2012.

Shields, Sarah. *Turkey*. Washington, DC: National Geographic, 2009.

On the Internet

Kids and Cultures: "Children's Day in Turkey"
  http://www.youtube.com/watch?v=feIzcqXWcy4

Republic of Turkey, Ministry of Foreign Affairs: *Discovering Turkey—Experiencing Turkey*
  http://kids.mfa.gov.tr/kids

TIME for Kids: *Around the World*, "Turkey"
  http://www.timeforkids.com/destination/turkey

Works Consulted

Agence France-Presse. "Turkey Reduces Length of Compulsory Military Service." *Defense News*, October 21, 2013. http://www.defensenews.com/article/20131021/DEFREG01/310210039/

Aksel, İsmail. "Turkish Judicial System: Bodies, Duties And Officials." Ministry of Justice of Turkey, 2013. http://www.justice.gov.tr/judicialsystem.pdf

Arsu, Sebnem, and Dan Bilefsky. "Turkey Lifts Longtime Ban on Head Scarves in State Offices." *New York Times*, October 8, 2013. http://www.nytimes.com/2013/10/09/world/europe/turkey-lifts-ban-on-head-scarves-in-state-offices.html?_r=0

Arsu, Sebnem. "Turkish Police Detain 30 in Crackdown on Demonstrators." *New York Times*, July 16, 2013. http://www.nytimes.com/2013/07/17/world/europe/turkish-crackdown-on-demonstrators.html?_r=0

Bal, İdris. "The Turkish Model and the Turkic Republics." *Perceptions—Journal of International Affairs*. vol. 3, no. 3, September-November 1998. http://www.sam.gov.tr/wp-content/uploads/2012/01/idris_bal.pdf

BBC News Europe. "Turkey Profile." January 8, 2014. http://www.bbc.co.uk/news/world-europe-17994865

BBC News. "Turkey Agrees Death Penalty Ban." January 9, 2004. http://news.bbc.co.uk/2/hi/europe/3384667.stm

Blue Mosque. "History." http://www.bluemosque.co/history.html

Bozdoğan, Sibel, and Reşat Kasaba, eds. *Rethinking Modernity and National Identity in Turkey*. Seattle, WA: University of Washington Press, 1997.

Bruno, Greg. "Inside the Kurdistan Workers Party (PKK)." Council on Foreign Relations, October 19, 2007. http://www.cfr.org/turkey/inside-kurdistan-workers-party-pkk/p14576

CIA. "Turkey." *The World Factbook*, January 14, 2014. https://www.cia.gov/library/publications/the-world-factbook/geos/tu.html

Ciddi, Sinan. "Turkey's Dark Clouds for Election Year 2014." *The World Post*, August 8, 2013. http://www.huffingtonpost.com/sinan-ciddi/turkeys-dark-clouds-for-e_b_3719613.html

Cigeroglu, Cengiz (native of Turkey). Interview with the author, November 2, 2013.

Cigeroglu, Heather (American art teacher who has taught in Turkey). Interview with the author, November 2, 2013.

Eligür, Banu. *The Mobilization Of Political Islam In Turkey*. New York: Cambridge University Press, 2010.

Ercan, Levent (Turkish Consulate in New York employee). Email correspondence with the author, December 6, 2013.

Facaros, Dana, and Michael Pauls. *Turkey*. Northampton, MA: Cadogan Guides USA, 2009.

Finkel, Andrew. *Turkey: What Everyone Needs To Know*. New York: Oxford University Press, 2012.

Finn, Robert P. "Ataturk's World View." *Light Millennium*, Fall 2010. http://www.lightmillennium.org/2010_24th/robert_p_finn_ataturk_world_view.html

Gore, Rick. "Wrath of the Gods—Earthquake in Turkey." *National Geographic*. http://science.nationalgeographic.com/science/earth/the-dynamic-earth/anatolian-fault/

Heper, Metin, and Nur Bilge Criss. *The A To Z Of Turkey*. Lanham, MD: Scarecrow Press, Inc., 2010.

İnce, Başak. *Citizenship And Identity In Turkey*. London: I.B. Tauris & Co Ltd, 2012.

Irez, Olga. "Classic Menemen Recipe." Delicious Istanbul, March 5, 2012. http://www.deliciousistanbul.com/blog/2012/03/05/classic-menemen-recipe/

Islamic-arts.org. "Islamic Calligraphy 1450-1925—West." Islamic Arts & Architecture, March 14, 2011. http://islamic-arts.org/2011/islamic-calligraphy-1450-1925-west/

Istanbul Cevahir. "About Us." http://www.istanbulcevahir.com/en-EN/about-us/46.aspx

FURTHER READING

Istanbul.com, "Marbling (Ebru): One of the Oldest Decorative Paper Arts." March 18, 2010. http://english. istanbul.com/explore-istanbul/traditional/marblingebru-one-of-the-oldest-decorative-paper-arts

Kasaba, Resat, ed. *The Cambridge History Of Turkey, Volume 4: Turkey in the Modern World.* Cambridge, UK: Cambridge University Press, 2008.

Kes-Erkul, Aysu. "Neighborhood Effects and Reproduction of Poverty: A Social Housing Case from Turkey." *International Journal of Humanities and Social Science*, vol. 3, no. 20, December 2013. http://www.ijhssnet.com/journals/Vol_3_No_20_December_2013/15.pdf

Kinzer, Stephen. *Reset: Iran, Turkey, And America's Future.* New York: Times Books, 2010.

Lamont-Doherty Earth Observatory. "The North Anatolian Fault." Columbia University. http://www.ldeo. columbia.edu/tamam/tamam-background/the-north-anatolian-fault

Law Society of England and Wales. "Turkey." http://international.lawsociety.org.uk/ip/europe/582/profile

Ohio State University Department of History. "Mustafa Kemal Ataturk." http://ehistory.osu.edu/world/ PeopleView.cfm?PID=213

Pamuk, Humeyra. "Number of Syrian Refugees in Turkey Exceeds 600,000: Turkish Official." Reuters, October 21, 2013. http://www.reuters.com/article/2013/10/21/us-syria-crisis-turkey-refugees-idUSBRE99K04O20131021

Park, Bill. *Modern Turkey.* New York: Routledge, 2012.

Parkinson, Joe. "Turkey Unveils Changes to Military Obligations." *Wall Street Journal*, November 24, 2011. http://online.wsj.com/news/articles/SB10001424052970204443404577054432267092986

Quota Project. "Grand National Assembly in Turkey." July 1, 2013. http://www.quotaproject.org/uid/ countryview.cfm?country=223

Ravindran, Sandeep. "Turkey's New Undersea Tunnel Is Built to Resist Earthquakes." *National Geographic Daily News*, November 4, 2013. http://news.nationalgeographic.com/news/2013/11/131104-earthquake-proof-marmaray-tunnel-turkey-engineering/

Republic of Turkey Ministry of Culture And Tourism. "Biography of Atatürk." http://www.kultur.gov.tr/ EN,31350/biography-of-ataturk.html

Republic of Turkey Ministry of Foreign Affairs. "Turkish Citizens Living Abroad." http://www.mfa.gov.tr/ the-expatriate-turkish-citizens.en.mfa

Rutherford, Tristan, and Kathryn Tomasetti. *Istanbul & Western Turkey.* Washington, DC: National Geographic Society, 2011.

Saraçoglu, Cenk. *Kurds Of Modern Turkey.* London: I.B. Tauris & Co Ltd, 2011.

Smith, Roff. "Why Turkey Lifted Its Ban on the Islamic Headscarf." *National Geographic Daily News*, October 11, 2013. http://news.nationalgeographic.com/news/2013/10/131011-hijab-ban-turkey-islamic-headscarf-ataturk/

Swan, Susan. *Turkey.* New York: DK Publishing, 2003.

Taşpinar, Ömer. "Turkey: The New Model?" The Brookings Institution, April 2012. http://www.brookings. edu/research/papers/2012/04/24-turkey-new-model-taspinar

Today's Zaman. "Bosporus Strait Threatened by Pollution." September 30, 2008. http://www.todayszaman. com/newsDetail_getNewsById.action;jsessionid=1F6D861633F3ACB7BAD474D3BA9F1CBD?news Id=154686

Today's Zaman. "40 Percent of Turks Never Go on Holiday." September 8, 2008. http://www.todayszaman. com/newsDetail_getNewsById.action;jsessionid=496ECC2A1DD77BFCB8D185EB9ACB5D0B?news Id=152470

Turkish Coalition of America. "National Sovereignty Day and Children's Day." http://www.tc-america.org/ issues-information/turkish-history/national-sovereignty-and-childrens-day-678.htm

Turkish Cultural Foundation. "Turkish Marbling, Ebru." http://www.turkishculture.org/fine-art/visual-arts/marbling/turkish-marbling-ebru-564.htm

UNESCO. "Hattusha: The Hittite Capital." World Heritage List. http://whc.unesco.org/en/list/377

UNESCO. "Neolithic Site of Çatalhöyük." http://whc.unesco.org/en/list/1405

Wall Street Journal. "Headscarf Ban Relaxed in Turkey, But Row Wages On." November 3, 2010. http:// live.wsj.com/video/headscarf-ban-relaxed-in-turkey-but-row-rages-on/E612641E-BDD6-4271-BF6A-944F614368B5.html#!8C9A1986-FF9F-4B2C-A8D3-C26BD6815501

Watson, Ivan. "Dolphins Dodge Danger in the Bosphorus Strait." NPR, April 7, 2007. http://www.npr.org/ templates/story/story.php?storyId=9446805

Zalewski, Piotr. "The Kurds' Last Battle in Turkey: Teaching Kids Kurdish." *Atlantic*, May 9, 2013. http:// www.theatlantic.com/international/archive/2013/05/the-kurds-last-battle-in-turkey-teaching-kids-kurdish/275719/

Zeldin, Wendy. "Turkey: Controversial Education Reform Legislation Passed." Library of Congress, April 17, 2012. http://www.loc.gov/lawweb/servlet/lloc_news?disp3_l205403094_text

GLOSSARY

Anatolia (an-uh-TOH-lee-uh)—The peninsula that is located in western Asia, which makes up most of Turkey today.

architecture (AHR-ki-tek-cher)—The art of designing buildings or spaces, or the buildings or spaces that have been designed.

backgammon (BAK-gam-uhn)—A board game for two people, played with dice and pieces called checkers.

constitution (kon-sti-TOO-shuhn)—Body of rules that the government uses to make laws.

cuisine (kwi-ZEEN)—A style of cooking, or the food made in a certain style.

Cypriot (SIP-ree-uht)—A resident or native of Cyprus.

hydroelectric (hahy-droh-i-LEK-trik)—Related to the generation of electicity from the energy created by falling water.

kebab (kuh-BOB)—Meat that has been grilled on a skewer.

linden (LIN-duhn)—A tree with fragrant yellow flowers.

minority (mi-NAWR-i-tee)—A group of people that numbers less than half of the total.

mosque (MOSK)—A Muslim place of worship.

negotiate (ni-GOH-shee-eyt)—To deal or bargain.

population (pop-yuh-LEY-shuhn)—The total number of people living in an area.

prophet (PROF-it)—A person who speaks on behalf of God.

refugee (ref-yoo-JEE)—A person who has left his country to escape war, natural disaster, etc.

techno (TEK-noh)—A type of music with very fast beats.

tectonic (tek-TON-ik)—Related to the structure of the earth's crust.

textile (TEKS-tahyl)—Fabric or cloth that has been woven or knitted.

Turk—Any resident or native of Turkey.

INDEX

About the Author

Alicia Klepeis began her career at the National Geographic Society. A former geography teacher, Alicia's students did tai chi, made Ghanaian-style coffins, and created Balinese batik. She is the author of the kids' book *Africa*, and is currently working on another kids' book entitled *Francisco's Kite*, due to be released in 2015. She has also written dozens of articles for both children and adults in magazines such as *National Geographic Kids, Kiki, FACES,* and *Appleseeds.* Alicia's passion for travel has taken her from Sydney to Sumbawa to Singapore, though she now wants to add Turkey to the stamps in her passport. In the meantime, she is learning to cook Turkish food in her upstate New York kitchen.

TURKEY